Friendly Evangelism

"Barbara Walker Sowersby is a gifted minister who has taught evangelism for many years. Her practical teaching will help you communicate the good news of Jesus more clearly and effectively. As a Victory Bible College teacher in my Evangelism and Outreach courses, Barbara has assisted me multiple times in teaching and imparting into the lives of the students."

Greg Ford
Tulsa, Oklahoma

Written by
Barbara Walker Sowersby

Christian Literature & Artwork
A BOLD TRUTH Publication

Friendly Evangelism
Copyright © 2018 by Barbara Sowersby
ISBN 13: 978-0-9998051-6-9

International Outreach Ministries
jbsoutreach@yahoo.com

BOLD TRUTH PUBLISHING
(Christian Literature & Artwork)
606 West 41ˢᵗ, Ste. 4
Sand Springs, Oklahoma 74063
www.BoldTruthPublishing.com ▪ *beirep@yahoo.com*

Available from Amazon.com and other retail outlets. Orders by U.S. trade bookstores and wholesalers. Quantity sales special discounts are available on quantity purchases by corporations, associations, and others. For details, contact the publisher at the address above.

Colored cover art & overall book design by Aaron Jones.

Printed in the USA.
05 18   10 9 8 7 6 5 4 3 2 1

We would like to recognize and thank these Publiishers, for publishing and distributing the following versions of God's written Word.

> *The Lord gave the word: great was the company*
> *of those that published it. - Psalm 68:11 (KJV)*

Dedication

This book is dedicated to my friend Matilda Hawk, who was a great inspiration to me, showing me in action 'one-on-one' evangelism.

Also, I want to dedicate it to my husband, Jim Sowersby [the Bible Scholar]. He has been a tremendous help and blessing to me with his amazing knowledge of the Scriptures.

Contents

Contents

Introduction

It is the job of the Church to bring the light of the Gospel to the world. This is our commission from Jesus; therefore, we must do it. How did He set this up? He told the Church to *"Go therefore and make disciples of all the nations..." (Matthew 28:19)*. Jesus also said in *Acts 1:8* that He would send the Holy Spirit to empower us and to help us do the job. When you become aware of His calling on your life, you will find yourself looking for opportunities to witness.

Friendly Evangelism is simply caring about people and being friendly, and sharing what you know about Jesus as the Holy Spirit leads you in order to bring them the Gospel of Jesus Christ. (It's being open to the leading of the Holy Spirit concerning who to approach [with the Gospel] in a casual way, in your everyday activities.)

Jesus told us in *John 4:35* that the *"fields...are already white for harvest!"* He also tells us in *Matthew 9:37-38* that the *"harvest truly is plentiful, but the laborers are few"* and that we should *"pray the Lord of the harvest to send out laborers into His harvest."* This book is written as a training tool emphasizing those laborers. Every Christian is not called to the office of Evangelist, but every Christian needs to know how to bring a person to Jesus and then help them become part of a good local church if possible.

I have found that some Christians really want to bring people to salvation and disciple them, but they lack practical knowledge of the how to's. You will learn how to start quickly and easily without feeling overwhelmed or defeated. In following the steps provided, you will plant seed for your own success.

Christians do not have to be biblical scholars or do extensive memorization of Scriptures before they can begin leading people to the Lord. They can move into action today as a harvester of souls. There are many people who plant, and many who water, but Jesus told us in *John 4:35*—go into the harvest fields and reap!

You will learn step-by-step how to win the lost. You will have access to procedures in one-on-one soul winning you can apply immediately. I want to impart to you how easy it is to reach the goal of bringing people into the Kingdom of God. By learning practical tips, recognizing hindrances that keep you from moving out, and asking the Holy Spirit to lead you to people, you can begin to plant, water, and harvest souls for the Kingdom of God!

"When there is a desire to lead people to The Lord, The Holy Spirit will lead you to people who are ready to receive Him."

— *Barbara Walker Sowersby*

Chapter 1

WHAT IS THE HARVEST?

God is moving mightily over the earth in these last days before His triumphant return to gather His children to Himself. Every child of God I know is anticipating His soon return. We are all sensing the excitement of His coming!

We are to look for His return *(Titus 2:13)*. We are also to be looking for a harvest of souls. *Matthew 9:37-38* says, *"The harvest truly is plentiful, but the laborers are few. Therefore pray the Lord of the harvest to send out laborers into His harvest."*

In recent days, I have come to realize most people do not know what the "harvest" is. We have heard the word *"harvest"* used many different ways. However, the harvest of souls is the number one priority of the Father. It is His heartbeat. He wants us to be not only looking for the harvest, but also bringing it in.

Precisely what is the "harvest" Jesus was talking about? The "harvest" is people who are ready to receive Jesus

Friendly Evangelism

as their Lord and Savior. Jesus did not personally talk to everyone He came in contact with, only the people the Holy Spirit prompted Him to talk to, such as the woman at the well in *John 4:1-42.* The Holy Spirit can and will lead us to the harvest this same way.

There is a harvest of people who have had the Word of God sown into their lives through witnessing or in some other way. Perhaps other witnesses have come along to water those seeds. These are the people ready to be harvested for Jesus and make Him Lord of their lives. They only need guidance. *(See: Acts 8:26-40)*

■ ■ ■

The "harvest" is people who are ready to receive Jesus as their Lord and Savior.

What my ministry is doing today is part of the answer to that shortage of laborers. I have embarked on a mission to familiarize churches and Bible schools with what the harvest truly is and to provide training to produce skillful laborers.

This effort was never more graphically illustrated than in a London church I ministered in. An opportunity opened for me to hold several meetings there. Outreach took on a new meaning for this church during the time I was there. Wonderfully, their outreach team

2

caught the vision of the harvest and of being harvest-minded. They also adapted themselves to the teaching I gave on setting and keeping the goals of salvation, baptism of the Holy Spirit, and being led by the Holy Spirit to discern the needs of people.

When we embarked on an outreach in the neighborhood, God proved out everything I had taught them. Six people were born again in the one hour we visited the neighborhood close to the church. God confirmed His Word by convincing the outreach team there truly is a "harvest" in London!

This neighborhood outreach with volunteers was what the Pastor wanted to do, and it was successful.

Sometimes the Harvest is Spectacularly Displayed by God

For example when I was in Russia years ago God moved supernaturally everyday. I was asked to bring the Message of Jesus into the High Schools in St. Petersburg—most of those in attendance received salvation.

On a night train to Moscow, a priest approached my cabin complaining about my ministry in the schools. I explained I had told the students to go with their parents to church. I asked him if he had ever received salvation

Friendly Evangelism

and he said no, he had not. Then he received the prayer of salvation.

Another was in a park outside of my hotel; an elderly man who could not speak English understood what I said to him in English—and he received salvation. [This was proved out by my interpreter when she arrived. She asked him about it in Russian and he repeated to her what I had spoke to him about.

Another time was in a food market in Russia and a security guard kept following me through the store. I turned and asked him could i help him and if he needed prayer. I could see and sense conviction on his face. He accepted salvation and his countenance changed before my eyes.

Chapter 2
WHY DO WE HARVEST?

Reaching people is God's heart. *Second Peter 3:9* tells us God is *"not willing that any should perish but that all should come to repentance."* Let us reflect on the reason for this.

■ ■ ■

By sending His Son to redeem us, God demonstrated His desire to make a way for all to be saved from Satan's hell.

God created the first man, Adam, to fellowship with Him. God also created Adam to have choice, like we do. When Adam chose to sin by disobeying God and listening to Satan, a gap was created between God and Adam. His disobedience also created a gap between God and the rest of mankind born of Adam. This disobedience, or sin, gave Satan a legal right to Adam and mankind thereafter. Therefore, sin became the separation between God and all of mankind.

God could not bear to have this continue. He sent His

Friendly Evangelism

Son, Jesus, to die on the cross and to be raised from the dead to wipe away the sin and bridge the gap created by the first man, Adam. By sending His Son to redeem us, God demonstrated His desire to make a way for all to be saved from Satan's hell. He made a way for all to have fellowship with Him!

Chapter 3
NATURAL WHEAT FIELD HEART OF MAN COMPARISON

People are in many stages of spiritual growth. The Holy Spirit knows which stage every individual is in at any given moment.

As we talk to people, showing concern and compassion for them, the Holy Spirit will reveal to us (confirm) which stage they are in by what they say or do.

Many people plow, plant, and water the seed of the Word; as a result more and more people are needed to bring in The Harvest of people needing salvation.

In *John 4:35,* Jesus compared the heart of man to a field. More than likely, it was a wheatfield. Let us compare the stages of natural growth of wheat to the spiritual growth of the human heart. Also, for further understanding, read *Mark 4:1-20.*

Friendly Evangelism

Natural Wheat Field	Heart of Man
Soil is Prepared *Field is plowed* *Weeds removed* *Nutrients added*	Heart Softened *Receives prayer and* *Christian kindness*
Seed is Sown *Planting seed in* *ground*	The Word of God is Sown *Receives encouraging* *Scripture*
Watered *Rain or irrigation*	Learns of Jesus *Receives more of the* *Word of God pertain-* *ing to the person*
Cultivated *Weeds are removed*	Is Stirred by the Holy Spirit *Doubts removed*
Harvest *Crop is brought in for* *use*	Salvation *Receives Jesus as Lord* *and Savior*

Chapter 4
Preparation Steps

■ 1. Ask God for His Love and Compassion for People

Everything we need can be obtained by asking God in prayer and receiving it in faith. God is love and He spreads His love abroad in our hearts by the Holy Spirit. We activate His love for people in our hearts by asking Him for a desire to see people come to Christ. God is a gentleman and He does not force His benefits on us. Jesus operated with compassion for people. He was able to do this by spending time with His Heavenly Father.

■ 2. Come Against Fear and Pride

Fear and pride are the two main reasons people do not talk to others about the Lord. Instead of stepping out, we fear what people will think and say about us. We feel we will be rejected and therefore do not make the effort. Pride is sometimes hidden under the guise of shyness. In some cases, being shy or reserved can mean we want to look perfect in the eyes of others. *Galatians 1:10* says we are to be pleasers of God and not pleasers of men.

Friendly Evangelism

■ 3. Spend Time with God in Bible Study and Prayer

We must cultivate a relationship with Him. In order to know God and recognize His Voice, we have to spend time with Him. Get to know the three Persons of the Trinity—the Father, the Son, and the Holy Spirit. They are three separate Persons in One. We make our requests to the Father in the Name of Jesus. We can also speak to Jesus about what He did on Earth. Jesus said He would send us a Helper—the Holy Spirit.

As we read the Bible, we get to know God's character. We also learn how Jesus did the works of the Father while on Earth and how He has sent the Holy Spirit to do those same works through us. And even *"greater works than these"* Jesus said we would do in *John 14:12*!

■ 4. Get to Know the Holy Spirit

The Holy Spirit is our helper. He helps us to fellowship with our Heavenly Father and with Jesus, His Son. It is the Holy Spirit Who will lead and guide us to people who need to hear about Jesus if we are open to His leading. He will also show us the needs of these people. That is why it is essential that we trust in Him.

We must first realize the Holy Spirit is inside us. We need to have this revelation and recognize the purpose for which He has been sent to us. He is our Helper.

Friendly Evangelism

He does not "do it all" for us. His job is to guide us and then to bring conviction to the lost soul. His job is supernatural! Our job is in the natural. We only put action to what He has asked us to do. But He puts the supernatural into action!

The Holy Spirit is the only One Who knows the hearts of people. He will set up divine appointments for us to meet them. What an exciting time it is to see Him work for us. I like to give my example of a movie production. In a movie production, there is a producer, a director, and a script. In our divine appointments, the Holy Spirit is the producer, and we are the director. We direct as He leads, but He is the One Who has the power to produce the results. Also in the script, the Holy Spirit will tell you the person's need. Oh, how exciting! I call this having an adventure with the Holy Spirit. I have had many adventures with Him. He never ceases to amaze me.

■ ■ ■

In order to know God and recognize His Voice, we have to spend time with Him. Get to know the three Persons of the Trinity— the Father, the Son, and the Holy Spirit.

The Holy Spirit knows certain details about the person long before you meet that person. He knows the

11

extent of the person's knowledge of the Word of God. He knows whether other laborers have already planted seed of God's Word in the person's heart. He knows if those seeds have been watered. And He knows whether or not the person is ready to receive Jesus as Lord and Savior. We must always be ready to hear His Voice so we know how to minister! We hear Him by a peaceful knowing inside us.

Most people I have led to the Lord are strangers to me. It is not necessary to know a person before approaching them. Ask the Holy Spirit for wisdom and discernment to know which stage of growth they are in. Usually, He will reveal it to you in what the person says and in the answers given to your questions. Listen carefully. Knowledge should be gained and used.

Different people I have led to the Lord told me they had already heard the Word of God from some other avenue. Others explained that someone close to them had been praying for laborers to come into their lives. Others said they themselves were praying and asking questions of God.

After we ask the Holy Spirit to lead us to people, we need to remember the goal of salvation and the Baptism of the Holy Spirit. This is very important! However, if for some reason the person is not ready to receive

Jesus as Savior, then you have the chance to plant seed in the person's heart; always be respectful of the person's right of choice. If you sense there is already seed planted by another—then water by giving encouragement from the Word of God if the person will allow you! The Holy Spirit is going to be your guide. Familiarize yourself with Him, and get to know Him.

John 16:13-15
"However, when He, the Spirit of truth, has come, He will guide you into all truth; for He will not speak on His own authority, but whatever He hears He will speak; and He will tell you things to come. He will glorify Me, for He will take of what is Mine and declare it to you. All things that the Father has are Mine. Therefore I said that He will take of Mine and declare it to you."

John 15:26-27
"But when the Helper comes, whom I shall send to you from the Father, the Spirit of truth who proceeds from the Father, He will testify of Me. And you also will bear witness, because you have been with Me from the beginning."

■ 5. Ask the Holy Spirit Daily to Lead You to a Person

As we spend time with the Holy Spirit, we become

more sensitive to what God wants. If we ask, He will put people in our path who need to hear about Jesus. Our job is to ask God for these people, and to be prepared to lead them to salvation as Jesus did. We need to watch and to be ready for opportunities; although, we do not want to force something to happen. When the Holy Spirit shows you someone, there will be a knowing in your spirit. He may point someone out to you, or He may call your attention to a certain person. This can happen before, during, or after you begin talking with the person.

■ ■ ■

If we ask, He will put people in our path who need to hear about Jesus.

You may notice someone in the same place you are in. Wait for an opportune time to talk with the person. Let the Holy Spirit work with you and lead you. Be wise in how you approach people. Always start by being friendly. Then, the Holy Spirit has something to work with.

Always prove out your leading by testing the waters. In other words, you will know as you go along whether the person is interested or not. The Holy Spirit will show you as you step out in faith. (See Practical Tips, beginning on page 23.)

14

Friendly Evangelism

■ 6. Learn Helpful Scriptures

Knowing Scriptures does not necessarily mean memorizing them or their location in the Bible. As long as you are familiar with a few encouraging Scriptures and some Scriptures on salvation, you will do just fine. The Holy Spirit will bring the appropriate Scripture to your remembrance when you need it.

I really believe the whole world can be won with just two or three Scriptures. This may shock you, but the fact is I normally use a paraphrased version of *John 14:6* and *Revelation 3:20.* At the right moment I will tell the person, *"Jesus said, 'No one comes to the Father except through Me. I stand at the door of your heart and knock. If you will let me in, I'll come in!'"* Remember, if the Holy Spirit has led you to someone who is part of the harvest, then he or she is ready to receive salvation!

Listed below are a few Scriptures to help you in getting started. *Jeremiah 29:11* is an excellent Scripture for encouragement. It can be used for anyone, especially young people. You will want to use a Scripture that fits the person's situation. Remember to not quote the Scripture by book, chapter, and verse. This can intimidate an unsaved person. Be willing to paraphrase—use your own words. This comes across as natural.

Friendly Evangelism

Encouraging Scriptures

1 Samuel 16:7
"the Lord looks at the heart."

Psalms 18:2
"The Lord is my rock and my fortress and my deliverer..."

Psalms 37:4
"Delight yourself also in the Lord, and He shall give you the desires of your heart."

Psalms 118:6
"The Lord is on my side; I will not fear. What can man do to me?"

Isaiah 43:19
"Behold, I will do a new thing..."

Jeremiah 29:11
"For I know the thoughts that I think toward you, says the Lord, thoughts of peace and not of evil, to give you a future and a hope."

Matthew 6:33
"Seek ye first the kingdom of God and His righteous-

Friendly Evangelism

ness, and all these things shall be added to you."

Matthew11:28-30
"Come to Me, all you who labor and are heavy laden, and I will give you rest. Take My yoke upon you and learn from Me, for I am gentle and lowly in heart, and you will find rest for your souls. For My yoke is easy and My burden is light."

John 10:10
"The thief does not come except to steal, and to kill, and to destroy. I have come that they may have life, and that they may have it more abundantly."

John 14:1
"Let not your heart be troubled; you believe in God, believe also in Me."

Philippians 4:6-7
"Be anxious for nothing, but in everything by prayer and supplication, with thanksgiving, let your requests be made known to God; and the peace of God, which surpasses all understanding, will guard your hearts and minds through Christ Jesus."

Colossians 3:15
"let the peace of God rule in your hearts…"

Friendly Evangelism

Hebrews 13:5
"For He Himself has said, 'I will never leave you nor forsake you.'"

Salvation Scriptures

John 3:1-8
"There was a man of the Pharisees named Nicodemus, a ruler of the Jews. This man came to Jesus by night and said to Him, 'Rabbi, we know that You are a teacher come from God; for no one can do these signs that You do unless God is with him.' Jesus answered and said to him, 'Most assuredly, I say to you, unless one is born again, he cannot see the kingdom of God.' Nicodemus said to Him, 'How can a man be born when he is old? Can he enter a second time into his mother's womb and be born?' Jesus answered, 'Most assuredly, I say to you, unless one is born of water and the Spirit, he cannot enter the kingdom of God. That which is born of the flesh is flesh, and that which is born of the Spirit is spirit. Do not marvel that I said to you, 'You must be born again.' The wind blows where it wishes, and you hear the sound of it, but cannot tell where It comes from and where it goes. So is everyone who is born of the Spirit.'"

Friendly Evangelism

John 14:6
"Jesus said to him, 'I am the way, the truth, and the life. No one comes to the Father except through Me."

Romans 3:10
"There is none righteous, no, not one..."

Romans 3:23
"for all have sinned and fall short of the glory of God."

Romans 5:8
"But God demonstrates His own love toward us, in that while we were still sinners, Christ died for us."

Romans 5:12
"Therefore, just as through one man sin entered the world, and death through sin, and thus death spread to all men, because all sinned..."

Romans 6:23
"For the wages of sin is death, but the gift of God is eternal life in Christ Jesus our Lord."

Romans 10:9-10
"If you confess with your mouth the Lord Jesus and believe in your heart that God has raised Him from the dead, you will be saved. For with the

Friendly Evangelism

heart one believes unto righteousness, and with the mouth confession is made unto salvation."

Romans 10:11-13
"For the Scripture says, 'Whoever believes on Him will not be put to shame, for there is no distinction between Jew and Greek, for the same Lord over all is rich to all who call upon Him.'"

2 Corinthians 6:2
"For he says: 'In an acceptable time I have heard you, and in the day of salvation I have helped you.' Behold, now is the accepted time; behold, now is the day of salvation."

Ephesians 2:8-10
"For by grace you have been saved through faith, and that not of yourselves; it is the gift of God, not of works, lest anyone should boast. For we are His workmanship, created in Christ Jesus for good works, which God prepared beforehand that we should walk in them."

Revelations 3:20
"Behold, I stand at the door and knock. If anyone hears My voice and opens the door, I will come in to him and dine with him, and he with Me."

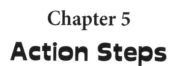

Chapter 5

Action Steps

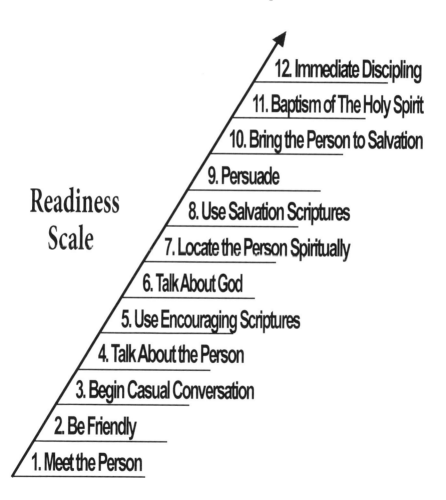

Readiness Scale

12. Immediate Discipling

11. Baptism of The Holy Spirit

10. Bring the Person to Salvation

9. Persuade

8. Use Salvation Scriptures

7. Locate the Person Spiritually

6. Talk About God

5. Use Encouraging Scriptures

4. Talk About the Person

3. Begin Casual Conversation

2. Be Friendly

1. Meet the Person

Friendly Evangelism

These steps are simply a guide. Depending on the person's readiness, you may be able to skip some steps. The Holy Spirit will guide you by what the person says.

■ 1. Meet the Person

Since you have asked the Holy Spirit to lead you to people who need to hear about Jesus, it will happen. You will have that knowing in your spirit—that still small voice. This will happen during everyday activities like running errands, shopping, standing in lines in public places that would be ordinarily boring. We need to be in tune with the Holy Spirit.

When you do find someone to talk to, do not become overly concerned as to whether it is the right person or not. Wait for an opportunity to test it out. Always be harvest-minded while you are talking to this person.

People ask me, *"Well, how do I know I am being led to a person?"* Sometimes it is as though the Holy Spirit is pointing to that person. Other times, I have had people walk up to me and just hang around until it became obvious to me that the Holy Spirit had put them in my path. Some people practically ask to be saved. And other times, you may know simply because you have been friendly to them and now they are responding to you. This will be noticeable to you if you are watching carefully. And it will be a pleasant surprise when you first experience it. The Lord will increase your faith and discernment as you step out. The Holy Spirit may prompt you to simply speak a word of encouragement.

■ 2. Be Friendly

In order to begin a conversation that may lead to salvation, we must be friendly. Greet the person first—then pause. This helps you to avoid appearing anxious. Be willing to go out of your way to make the person feel comfortable.

Try to be as relaxed as you can. You will improve with practice. People are more easily drawn to others who are relaxed in appearance. If you are a beginner, you probably do not feel relaxed. However, a serious or tense look could alarm a person.

And, remember to express joy! True joy comes from spending time with God, and it is contagious! Sometimes, however, our attitude is not what it should be. Since people easily pick up on our moods, we will need to exercise control. We have a choice to express a joyful attitude. Our positive words will override any negative mood. And our opportunities will be greater if our joy is apparent to those around us.

Friendly Evangelism

Always be friendly to everyone. Look for opportunities to give God's love to the people you meet. It is very important to edify the person you are led to. People do not care as much about what you say as they do about how much you care. Let them experience the love of God through you.

■ 3. Begin Casual Conversation

Find a common ground or something you know that is of interest to the person. It may be as simple as making a comment about what they are doing at the moment. In fact, the simpler—the better! This will not put the person on guard by giving them a clue as to your goal. What is your goal? To win them to Christ!

Look for an opportunity to talk to the person without drawing attention from others. You will want to talk to the person one-on-one without anyone else listening. There are exceptions, of course. Use discretion. If you are in a store or some other public place, carefully watch your surroundings. (For further information, see Practical Tips, beginning on page 23.)

■ 4. Talk About the Person

Personalize the conversation with the person. Ask for their name. Comment on something that pertains to them. In fact, if you see an obvious need concerning

24

Friendly Evangelism

them, then you have a perfect opportunity to start a conversation. Jesus did this with the woman at the well in *John 4:5-30*. He found something to talk about that was relevant to her situation.

If the person picks up on your conversation, keep talking. We can tell from the person's response how to move forward. I always tell people in my meetings to keep talking as long as the person is willing to talk and is interested in what you are saying. I have found that if you show interest in the person, you will pleasantly get their attention.

■ ■ ■

Our positive words will override any negative mood. And our opportunities will be greater if our joy is apparent to those around us.

People have asked me, *"If I start a conversation with someone I have just met, how do I know God wants me to tell them about Jesus?"* I say, *"That's easy! Do they keep talking to you?"* If the answer is, *"Yes,"* then probably God is leading you to tell the person about Jesus.

You are leading the conversation. Make it go the right way! As you keep talking to a person, sooner or later, the person will probably divulge a part of his or her life where there is a need, or something the person has been struggling with. Most Christians, at this point, tend to immediately want to stop and pray. Don't pray too soon! Don't be sidetracked by the person's need and forget your goal of salvation. Later, when you lead the person through a prayer of salvation, you can pray for his need.

Again, try to be relaxed. It is natural to become excited, especially if you sense the person is truly in need and possibly ready to meet Jesus. Control this tendency and you will stay on your course of success. The person who is lost does not have knowledge of your intentions. And it is important to maintain your goal. Many times, Christians scare people away by acting overly anxious. Take one step at a time! Make sure you have the person's full attention. This is very important! Without this, you cannot go another step. If you do not have their full attention, wait until you do. Be aware you probably have only a few minutes to reach your goal.

■ 5. Use Encouraging Scriptures

Turn the conversation Heavenward! Begin to apply encouraging Scripture to the person's need. Do not quote it by book, chapter, and verse. Put it in your own words—paraphrase it. You do not want to intimidate the person. (See list of Encouraging Scriptures, beginning on page 8.) You may want to use appropriate Scriptures that are already familiar to you.

■ 6. Talk About God

We have to work up to talking about the Lord and the Word of God concerning salvation. I am not saying you have to take a long time doing this. You don't have much time in a public place. A conversation can be started and you can end by leading them to Christ in five minutes or less. Many think this cannot be done. I have personally experienced this hundreds of times. And you thought you didn't have time to win the lost!

Remember to watch your surroundings at this point. Be sensitive to protect the person's dignity and comfort level. (See Practical Tips, beginning on page 47.)

■ 7. Locate the Person Spiritually

Locating a person spiritually is simply determining what the person believes and trusts in. You can locate a person by listening to what is said and how the person responds to your questions. What people say gives you a clue as to their beliefs and knowledge of God. This is how you discern their stage of readiness. Think about this as an investigation. You're investigating where people are spiritually. The Holy Spirit will confirm this to you as you talk.

Friendly Evangelism

The following questions can help you discern what a person believes and trusts in:

★ **A.** *"Do you ever get a chance to go to church, or do you have to work on Sundays?"* This is good to ask, especially if the person is working. (You are trying to find out whether he or she is going to church on Sundays.) And you will probably get a more honest answer than if you asked, *"Do you go to church?"* This puts a person on the defense. In a discrete way, find out if the person is attending church and what type of church it is. Don't look alarmed or make comments regardless of the answer. If the person does attend church, this lets you know he or she has an interest in the things of God. Also, it gives you some idea about what the person believes. You are encouraged to gain at least a minimal knowledge of the different religions and denominational churches in order to have an idea of different ideas and beliefs people may have about God.

★ **B.** *"Well, tell me. Where does God fit into your plans?"* This is a good question to ask if the person begins talking about his or her life—work, school, children, or anything else the person cares about.

This question is vital and should be used with or without the first two questions. If you discern a person is ready to meet Jesus immediately, you can go straight to this question:

Friendly Evangelism

★**A.** *"Let me ask you something. Are you hoping to go to Heaven, or do you know for sure you're going?"* The person's response to this question will tell you about his or her spiritual condition. This is a foundational step in turning the conversation toward salvation.

★**B.** If you sense the person isn't quite ready, you can add this question, *"If you died and went to the Gates of Heaven today and God asked you, 'Why should I let you in?' what would you say? God would say to you, 'Did you receive My Son Jesus, or did you reject Him?'"* Then tell the person, *"The only way into Heaven is to receive Jesus."*

These questions show your compassion for the person. The responses given will tell you about the person's spiritual condition. Stating these questions this way does not come across as intimidating.

[You can watch the eyes of the person you are talking with to know if they are interested or not. Their body language can also tell you if they want to listen any further.]

■ 8. Use Salvation Scriptures

At this point, you are ready to say, *"Jesus said, 'No one comes to the Father except through Me. I stand at the door of your heart and knock. If you'll let me in, I'll come in.'"* Notice this is a paraphrased version of two

Friendly Evangelism

Scriptures, *John 14:6* and *Revelation 3:20*. (To familiarize yourself with the salvation plan, see list of Salvation Scriptures on pages 15 and 20.)

■ 9. Persuade

At some point, the person will be hit by the convicting power of God. You'll notice it in their face when this happens. I call it *"being arrested by the Holy Spirit."* That's when it is time to ask, *"Would you like to ask Jesus into your heart—right now?"* Pause before you say right now. This is important. It puts an urgency in what you are saying. If they respond positive, do not hesitate to pray.

If the person feels under pressure for time, let him know it only takes seconds. Say, *"You can know you are going to Heaven right now. You don't have to bow down or close your eyes. No one has to know what we are doing. It will only take 10 to 20 seconds."* Sometimes people will indicate to you that they want to put this off for "someday." Remind them of the passage in the Bible that says, *"Now is the day of salvation"* (2 Corinthians 6:2).

■ 10. Bring the Person to Salvation

Lead the person in a prayer of salvation. This can be a prayer in your own words as long as they ask Jesus into their heart to be Lord and Savior over their life. Below is an example of a prayer of salvation:

Friendly Evangelism

Father, I know You sent Your Son Jesus to die on the cross. I believe You raised Him from the dead. Jesus, come into my heart. Be my Lord and my Savior! Amen.

Also, remember to pray for any other needs the person mentioned during the conversation. And, if time allows, give thanks to the Lord for giving the new believer assurance that he or she is saved.

After the prayer, I will ask the person, *"Who has been praying for you?"* Almost always, the person will say that a grandmother, mother, some family member, or a close friend has been praying for them. I know that if God calls me to talk to a person, it is because someone, somewhere, has been praying for that person!

■ 11. Baptism of the Holy Spirit

The best time for a new believer to receive the Baptism of the Holy Spirit is right away. The new believer is more open to the infilling of the Holy Spirit at this time than at any other time. I did not know this until the Lord began to deal with me about it.

As soon as you finish a prayer of salvation, say to the person, *"Now, there's a power you need!"* Then, tell the person the benefits of that power by saying:

Friendly Evangelism

▶1. *"It will help you to understand the Bible in a way you never have before."* I tell the person, *"This is what happened to me."*

▶2. I say, *"This power will give you your own Heavenly language from the Lord.*

▶3. *"It will help you to pray for your family and others when you don't know how to pray.*

▶4. *"It will charge you up with power just like a battery is charged with power!*

▶5. *"It will give you joy and boldness."*

Then I say, *"Would you like to have that power? It will only take a few seconds."* If the person responds with *"Yes,"* I say, *"Then, repeat after me: Jesus, baptize me with the precious Holy Spirit."* At this time, I explain that I will be praying for a few seconds in my Heavenly language. I also explain, *"You will receive a syllable or a word of your own language, but you will have to speak it out using your own voice and tongue."* When I see the person's mouth move, I encourage him or her by saying, *"That's it! Keep going!"* Then, I encourage the person, saying, *"Keep praying daily for God to add to your language. This will give you the spiritual empowerment you need for a lifetime!"* If the person does not speak a word or syl-

Friendly Evangelism

lable, I say, *"Just keep thanking God for the baptism and you will soon receive your Heavenly language."*

Leading someone in prayer for the Baptism can happen in public just as easily as leading the person to salvation. I didn't know it was possible until I tried it myself. I am the last person who would want to cause a scene in public, but I found if I take all the same precautions with this step as I do leading the person to the Lord, he or she feels secure and we both remain relaxed. I protect the person in the same way; by watching my surroundings, taking care not to call attention to what I am doing, and this prevents embarrassment.

■ ■ ■

Remember to watch your surroundings at this point. Be sensitive to protect the person's dignity and comfort level.

Do not worry if the first few people you pray for do not speak in tongues right away. Assure them that they will receive their Heavenly language. This happened to the first few people I prayed for. I was determined, though, and one day, the person spoke in tongues! It takes practice. As we step out in faith, the Lord brings increase. Your faith increases and so does the anointing!

Friendly Evangelism

<u>Baptism of the Holy Spirit Scriptures</u>

John 14:12-16
"Most assuredly, I say to you, he who believes in Me, the works that I do he will do also; and greater works than these he will do, because I go to My Father. And I will pray the Father, and He will give you another Helper, that He may abide with you forever..."

Acts 1:4-5
"And being assembled together with them, He commanded them not to depart from Jerusalem, but to wait for the Promise of the Father, "which," He said, "you have heard from Me; for John truly baptized with water, but you shall be baptized with the Holy Spirit not many days from now."

Acts 19:1-6
"...And finding some disciples he said to them, 'Did you receive the Holy Spirit when you believed?' So they said to him, 'We have not so much as heard whether there is a Holy Spirit.' And he said to them, 'Into what then were you baptized?' So they said, 'Into John's baptism.' Then Paul said, 'John indeed baptized with a baptism of repentance, saying to the people that they should believe on Him who would come after him, that is, on Christ Jesus.' When they heard this, they were baptized in the

name of the Lord Jesus. And when Paul had laid hands on them, the Holy Spirit came upon them, and they spoke with tongues and prophesied."

Acts 8:14-17
"Now when the apostles who were at Jerusalem heard that Samaria had received the Word of God, they sent Peter and John to them, who, when they had come down, prayed for them that they might receive the Holy Spirit. For as yet He had fallen upon none of them. They had only been baptized in the name of the Lord Jesus. Then they laid hands on them, and they received the Holy Spirit."

■ 12. Immediate Discipling

Somewhere in the conversation you have learned the person's name. Write it down. And, if at all possible, get his or her phone number. Below are listed some steps the new believer will need to take in order to grow as a Christian. But, help the person to see serving God as desirable instead of a task. Encourage the new believer to see the benefits of following the Lord in these five ways:

▶ **1. To become involved in a good church.** Invite the person to your own church. Tell him or her what your church has done for you. Plan to meet the new believer at the door of the church, or if possible, offer a ride the first time. If the person is of the opposite sex, you will want to find a person of the same gender in your congregation to do this for you.

If the person is not from your area, do whatever is reasonable to help him or her. If time allows, a phone directory is helpful. You can tell the person, *"You need to be in a place where people will love and encourage you. You need to be in a church where you can learn about Jesus."*

▶ **2. To pray to the Father in Jesus' Name for needs.** Explain that praying is the same as talking to God.

▶ **3. To read the Bible.** *The Book of John* is a good place to start—one chapter a day.

▶ **4. To give their testimony to someone they trust.** This may be the person who prayed for them.

▶ **5. To understand there is an enemy who will try to discourage them.** Explain to the believer, *"This is why you need to be in a good church, to pray and to read your Bible. John 10:10 says, 'The thief does not come except to steal, and to kill, and to destroy. I have come that you may have life, and that you may have it more abundantly.'"*

36

Chapter 6
EXAMPLES OF DIALOGUE FOR THE HARVEST

EXAMPLE 1:

You meet a person and begin casual conversation. You ask her a question that pertains to her life. This may be about her family, school, work, etc. As she responds to you, your conversation can go as follows:

Barbara: *"Tammy, I can see you are a very busy lady. You work and take care of your children. Can I ask, 'Where does God fit into your life?'"*

Tammy: *"Well, I don't know. He used to be a big part of my life. And now, I don't even know if He cares about me anymore."* (Listen to the response. This will help you locate the person spiritually.)

Barbara: *"Tammy, He does care about you. He still loves you very much. He sent His Son Jesus so that you would know how much He loves you."*

Friendly Evangelism

Tammy: *"Well, I guess so."*

Barbara: *"Tammy, are you hoping to go to Heaven, or do you know for sure you're going?"*

Tammy: *"Well, I hope I'm going to Heaven."* [This response lets you know the person desires to be saved.]

Barbara: *"You don't have to hope. You can know for sure—right now. It will only take about 20 seconds! Jesus said, 'No one comes to the Father except through Me. I stand at the door of your heart and knock. If you'll let me in, I'll come in!' Would you like to receive Jesus into your heart—right now?"*

Tammy: *"Yes, I would!"*

Barbara: *"You can just repeat a prayer after me. You don't have to bow down or close your eyes.*

'Father, I know You sent Your Son Jesus to die on the cross. I believe You raised Him from the dead. Jesus, come into my heart. Be my Lord and my Savior! Give me the assurance I am going to Heaven. Amen.'"

This prayer is to be repeated by the person, one sentence at a time as you say it with feeling.

Friendly Evangelism

<u>**EXAMPLE 2:**</u>

You are in a public work place and begin casual conversation with an employee. The dialogue could go as follows:

Barbara: *"I see you are a hard worker. Do you work on Sunday's too?"*

Sam: *"Sometimes."*

Barbara: *"Well, tell me. Do you ever get a chance to go to church on Sunday's?"*

Sam: *"Sometimes."*

Barbara: *"Are you hoping to go to Heaven, or do you know for sure you're going?"*

Sam: *"I know I'm going."*

Barbara: *"Can I ask how you know? Did someone pray with you as a child or later?"*

Sam: *"Well, no. But, I've always tried to be good and do what's right. My parents took me to church."*

Barbara: *"You know, Sam, no one can be good*

Friendly Evangelism

enough to get to Heaven. It's by grace, not by works. Jesus said, 'No one comes to the Father except through Me. I stand at the door of your heart and knock. If you'll let me in, I'll come in.' Would you like to receive Jesus into your heart—right now? No one has to know what we're doing. You don't have to bow down or shut your eyes. It will only take about 20 seconds."

Sam: *"Yes! I would!"*

Barbara: *"Just say, 'Father, I know you sent Your Son Jesus to die for me on the cross. I believe in my heart that He was raised from the dead. Jesus, come into my heart. Be my Lord and my Savior.   Amen.'"*

EXAMPLE 3:

You are in a bookstore, and you begin casual conversation with a lady. You ask her a question that pertains to her. The conversation can go as follows:

Barbara: "I see you like to read books about cooking."

Sara: "Yes, I do!"

Barbara: "Are there any really good recipes in there?"

40

Friendly Evangelism

Sara: "Yes, there are. But, I don't cook much any-more."

Barbara: *"Oh! Why not?"*

Sara: *"Well, I used to cook for my husband all the time. But, he just passed away."*

Barbara: *"Oh! I'm so sorry! I know this is a hard time for you. Do you have people in your life who can be of support to you at this time?"*

Sara: *"Not really."*

Barbara: *"Well, Sara, I know one thing. God loves you and He wants to be of support. Tell me something. Are you hoping to go to Heaven, or do you know you're going?"*

Sara: *"No, I'm not!"*

Barbara: *"What makes you say that?"*

Sara: *"Well, I've just done a lot of things that were really bad."*

Barbara: *"You know, Sara? No matter what you've done, God loves you. And Jesus comes to meet you* *right where you are. You don't have to be good enough to receive Him. No one is good enough. Jesus said, 'No one comes to the Father, except through Me. I stand at the door of your heart and knock. If you'll let me in, I'll come in. Would you like to receive Jesus into your heart—right now?"*

Sara: *"Yes! I would!"*

Barbara: *"Just say, 'Father, I know You sent Your Son Jesus to die for me on the cross. I believe in my heart that He was raised from the dead. Jesus, come into my heart. Be my Lord and my Savior. Give me assurance that I'm going to Heaven. Amen.'"*

EXAMPLE 4:

You are in a store and overhear someone cry out to God. Immediately you discern the person is ready to meet Jesus. Your conversation can go as follows:

Susie: *"I just can't go on. I need God!"*

[You turn to this woman and begin to talk with her]

Barbara: *"Well, we all need God! He sent His Son Jesus to help us. Are you hoping to go to Heaven, or*

Friendly Evangelism

do you know you are going?"

Susie: *"I don't know!"*

Barbara: *"Well, Susie, you don't have to guess. You can know for sure in about 20 seconds. You don't have to bow down or close your eyes. Would you like to receive Jesus in your heart—right now?"*

Susie: *"Yes! I would!"*

Barbara: *"Just say, 'Father, I know You sent Your Son Jesus to die for me on the cross. I believe in my heart that He was raised from the dead. Jesus, come into my heart. Be my Lord and my Savior. Give me assurance that I'm going to Heaven. Amen.'"*

Friendly Evangelism

Chapter 7

Testimony

O nce, while I was ministering in a London church and teaching on these concepts, the people caught the vision of the harvest and of being harvest-minded.

When we embarked on an outreach in the neighborhood, God proved out everything I had just taught them. The Pastor and I visited an apartment building where I knocked on a door. A sleepy young man answered. (**<u>Meeting the person</u>.**) Obviously, I had awakened him. After apologizing for disturbing him, I invited him to the church that I was ministering in. (**<u>Being friendly and starting conversation</u>.**) When I asked him if he went to church anywhere, he replied that he did not, but knew he should be going. (**I began talking about him and he responded well. This was <u>my opening to continue</u>.**) He told me that at one time he wanted to be a priest. (**<u>This gave me a clue as to his location spiritually</u> since I could see God had been dealing with this young man for a long time.**) I told him it was not by chance that I was there. (**I turned the**

45

conversation toward God.) I asked him, *"Are you hoping to go to Heaven, or do you know for sure that you are going?"* He said, *"I hope I am going!"* (**At this point, I had located him spiritually. I also knew he would accept the Lord.**) When I told him he didn't have to hope and that he could know for sure in about 20 seconds, he looked at me as if to say, *"Really?"* I answered his questioning eyes saying, *"Yes, really. You can know for sure. Jesus said, 'No one comes to the Father except through Me. I stand at the door of your heart and knock. If you will let Me in, I will come in.'"* (**Using Scripture.**) He just stood there staring at me. (**I could see as I gave him these portions of Scripture that the Holy Spirit had arrested him.**) Quickly, I asked him, *"Would you like to ask Jesus into your heart right now?"* (**Persuasion.**) He said, *"Yes, I would."* I had him repeat a salvation prayer. (**Bring him to salvation.**) He invited us in to pray for his family. Beyond that, he started coming to church the following Sunday.

Chapter 8
Practical Tips

How to Recognize the Harvest

I have been asked many times, *"How do I know they are the harvest?"* I will ask, *"Does the person keep talking to you? Are they interested?"* If the answer is *"yes,"* then you are probably led to speak to that person.

If while you are talking to someone you sense The Lord wants you to locate them spiritually, it's important that you don't hesitate. Never forget your goal (leading them to Christ), keep that in mind the entire time you talking to them.

Some people are like a fish that jumps onto your line! Others shut you out. Remember, if a person does not continue the conversation with you, that one is not the harvest. Leave those people alone. And do not feel guilty believing that you have somehow failed. We cannot go past what the Holy Spirit wants. If we do, we are taking liberties. We must show respect for all people by not going any further than they want to go.

Friendly Evangelism

If a person becomes argumentative or defensive in any way, it is a sign that person is not ready. I will say, *"I can see that I'm not going to answer your questions to your satisfaction,"* and I will drop the subject politely.

The enemy wants us to feel defeated. Many people give up and vow never to witness again because they tried to push through with a person who did not want to talk, much less be saved. Don't be discouraged if this happens. We can establish whether we have been led by the Holy Spirit by observing and listening to people talk. We do not need to proceed with people who aren't ready. There are plenty of people out there who are. They not only need what you have, they want it!

■ Watch Your Surroundings

Many people I talk to will not realize how loud they are talking. I will discreetly let them know others are listening and that they need to lower their voice. You will want to protect everyone's dignity. Also, avoid whispering. Whispering peaks the interest of others around you. If a person should realize others are listening and suddenly become embarrassed, the person may abruptly end the conversation with you, putting an end to your opportunity.

If you are witnessing to someone while he or she is

48

working, be appreciative of the employer's time. You do not want to put someone's job in jeopardy. Assess the situation and act as quickly as possible without looking hurried. Most employees can talk for a minute or two if they have no customers or tasks to be completed. Many times I wait while the person takes care of a customer. Then, I finish my conversation with him or her.

■ Anticipate Distractions and Interruptions

Another reason to watch your surroundings is to be aware of possible distractions and interruptions. When I am witnessing to a person in a public place and I notice someone coming close, I will pause and stop talking and stare at the person approaching until they pass by. Do what you need to do in order to not draw attention to the situation. The devil will sometimes send distractions from others around you. You can control what happens. Keep things on track.

■ ■ ■

We do not need to proceed with people who aren't ready. There are plenty of people out there who are. They not only need what you have, they want it!

If we can alleviate embarrassment, discomfort, and fears, we will earn the trust of those we witness to and they will be more open to talk to us. This can mean the difference between success and failure!

■ Get to the Point; It's a Timing Thing

I have heard about and even witnessed many people start talking to a person and get them to the point where it is obvious they would accept salvation, only to lose the opportunity. What did they do wrong? They kept talking, and talking—and talking about salvation until the person had to go or they were interrupted by circumstances or other people.

That's why you have to hurry with them and get to the true purpose of your conversation. Now at the same time you don't want to appear to be rushed, but just know: often they will only have a few minutes to visit, and for you to reach the goal of getting them saved.

■ Keep Your Eye on the Goal

You are there to get them: to pray with you and receive Jesus Christ as their Savior and maybe the baptism in The Holy Spirit. Then if time permits exchange some follow-up information with them and possibly give them some more instructions about their new life as a Christian. If you only get to the first one, you have won a soul and accomplished much good.

Chapter 9
Jump Start Outline
Steps to Win the Lost

■ **PREPARATION STEPS:**

▶ **1.** Ask God for His love and compassion for people. *John 3:16; Galatians 3:12-14.*

▶ **2.** Come against all fear and pride. *2 Timothy 1:7; 1 Peter 5:5*

▶ **3.** Spend time with God in Bible study and prayer. *2 Timothy 2:15; Jude 20; John 14; John 15*

▶ **4.** Ask the Holy Spirit daily to lead you to a person. *Acts 18:5; John 6:63; John 16:13; 1 John 5:6*

▶ **5.** Learn salvation Scriptures. **Examples:** *Romans 3:10; 3:23; 5:12; 6:23; 5:8; 10:9,10; 10:11-13; John 3:1-8, Ephesians 2:8-10; 2 Corinthians 6:2; John 14:6; Revelation 3:20.*

■ **ACTION STEPS:** Always be relaxed, joyful and

Friendly Evangelism

friendly. *See Ephesians 4:32; Romans 12:10; Colossians 3:12.*

▪ WEEK 1:

Begin leaving tracts during your daily activities as God directs you. *Study James 1:22; James 1:5; Colossians 4:5.*

▪ WEEK 2:

Make friendly conversation while handing out tracts. *See Colossians 3:17.*

▪ WEEK 3:

Begin talking to people without the use of tracts. *See 1 Peter 3:15.*

▪ ASK THE QUESTION:

"Would you like to invite Jesus into your heart RIGHT NOW?"

Then, pray a salvation prayer.

Chapter 10
Jump Start

This is a plan to help the beginner ease into a lifestyle of leading people to Jesus. Sometimes beginners fear rejection from others. However, we must not fear man. *Proverbs 29:25* says, *"The fear of man brings a snare, but whoever trusts in the Lord will be safe."* Remember to ask the Holy Spirit for boldness!

I often tell a story about a child and his fear of water. A dad brought his child who had never been swimming before to the ocean and told his son to jump right in. Well, you can imagine the fear the child felt. First, the boy put his toes in to feel the temperature of the water. Then he stepped in with both feet. Soon, he felt comfortable enough to go in up to his knees and then to his waist. It takes time to get used to something new. It is no different with witnessing.

Following are some steps to help you become an effective witness for the Lord without feeling overwhelmed and defeated.

Friendly Evangelism

- Week 1:

Begin leaving tracts during your daily activities.

The first week, as you go about your daily activities, leave tracts in designated places. This can be done by anyone—experienced or not. Remember to always have tracts with you as you go about your daily activities. [**In the back of this book, We have provided 3 copies of the tract I like to use.**] Keep them available in your car, briefcase, organizer, purse, pockets, etc. There are many places to leave tracts beginning with restaurants. Leave one on the table with your tip for the waiter or waitress. As a word of caution—leave a tract only if you give the waiter or waitress a good tip. This is very important! Leaving a tract with little or no tip is a bad witness. A good tip is considered to be at least twenty percent of the price of your meal. If you are not able to leave this amount or more, do not leave a tract. There are other places to leave them, but use wisdom and discretion. Remember to always be sensitive to the prompting of the Holy Spirit.

In leaving tracts, you will be planting seed for your own success in personal evangelism. Doing this puts you in contact with a person and moves you toward your goal of winning the lost. Since everything comes by sowing and reaping and seedtime and harvest in the Kingdom of God, you have planted some of the best seed for yourself as well as for the person receiving the tract. The more you do this, the easier it becomes. And best of all, the person receiving the tract is learning about Jesus.

■ **Week 2:**

Make Friendly conversation while handing out tracts.

The second week, make small conversation while handing the tract to the person God puts on your heart. This step may seem scary at first, but that will change if you do not become overly anxious. Remember, the Holy Spirit is guiding you since you have already asked Him to take away fear and give you boldness. Begin by using minimal conversation. As you gain confidence, add more to your conversation. If you are in a restaurant, hand the tract to the waitress or waiter with your tip inside it and say something like, *"I would like for you to have this."* Or, *"Here is your tip."* Make sure, however, you place the tip inside the tract so it is obvious. In time, you will become more comfortable and able to say more to the person as you give him or her the tract.

Friendly Evangelism

- Week 3:

Begin talking to people without the use of tracts.

By week three, the tracts will have served their purpose in getting you started. You will feel comfortable enough to talk to people without relying on the tracts. You have gained experience in being led by the Holy Spirit to a person. As you step out in faith, you will begin to notice God's leading in a greater way. Do not forget to ask for God to lead you on a daily basis. You will be amazed at how He uses you. God will give you boldness and discernment as you ask Him.

About the Author

Barbara Walker Sowersby is a 1995 graduate of Rhema Bible College and has lived in the Tulsa, Oklahoma area for over 24 years.

Barbara and her husband Jim have been members of (A.F.C.M.) Associated Faith Churches and Ministries since 2000.

Barbara is a soul-winner and has a true love for people and a desire to rescue the lost and hurting, and see their lives transformed through the power of The Gospel Message.

She travels across America and other nations teaching believers from various churches and Bible Schools, to lead others to The Lord in everyday activities through "Friendly Evangelism." Barbara uses volunteers as play-actors to demonstrate and practice these witnessing techniques.

It's like the old saying, "Give a man a fish, and you feed him for a day. Teach him to fish, and you feed him for a lifetime."

Jesus said, "Follow me, and I will make you fishers of men." (Mat 4:19)

About the Author

Barbara and Jim are doing exactly that—teaching Jesus' followers around the world to be fishers of men.

It is a very effective method of impacting a community or even a whole city with The Gospel.

Currently, Barbara and Jim minister together as:
Jim and Barbara Sowersby
International Outreach Ministries

Enjoy these other great books from Bold Truth Publishing

Seemed Good to THE HOLY GHOST
by Daryl P Holloman

Effective Prison Ministries
by Wayne W. Sanders

TURN OFF THE STEW
by Judy Spencer

The Holy Spirit SPEAKS Expressly
by Elizabeth Pruitt Sloan

Matthew 4:4
Man shall not live by bread alone...
by Rick McKnight

VICTIM TO VICTOR (THE CHOICE IS YOURS)
by Rachel V. Jeffries

SPIRITUAL BIRTHING
Bringing God's Plans & Purposes and Manifestation
by Lynn Whitlock Jones

BECOMING PERFECT
Let The Perfector Perfect His Work In You
by Sally Stokes Weiesnbach

FIVE SMOOTH STONES
by Aaron Jones

Available at select bookstores and
www.BoldTruthPublishing.com

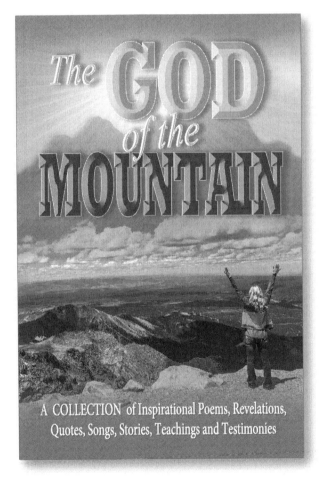

You can grow as a Christian:

❖ **Attend a Bible-believing church.**

❖ Read the Bible and learn about God and His principles.

(Example: Start with the book of John, one chapter at a time.)

❖ Turn from sinful living.

❖ Pray often to God in Jesus' name—Talk to God. Confess your sins; share your joys and problems. Thank God for your blessings.

❖ Tell others about your Savior.

You are invited to:

Place your Ministry or Church name here and use it as your own.

Permission is granted by the author to copy and use this "Do You Know for Sure?" brochure for ministry and personal use. Please do not reprint for commercial use or resale.

Do
You
Know
for Sure?

You Can Know Jesus

Jesus said,

"I am the way, the truth, and the life. No one comes to the Father except through me. . ." (John 14:6)

". . . I stand at the door and knock. If you let me in, I will come in. . . ." (Revelation 3:20)

Would you like to invite Jesus into your heart -- **Right now?**

Just say, **"Lord Jesus, come into my heart. Be my Lord and my Savior."**

1 Believe in your heart: that Jesus Christ is the Son of God; that He died for you on the cross; that he rose from the dead.

2 Then confess with your mouth that Jesus is your Lord and Savior.

3 You will be saved.

Romans10:9: If you confess with your mouth the Lord Jesus, and believe in your heart that God has raised him from the dead, you will be saved.

You can know **for sure** where you're going when you die.

God loves you and wants you to know that you're going to heaven when you die.

Everyone has sinned and come short of the glory of God. Sin has separated us from God.

Romans 3:23: For all have sinned, and come short of the glory of God.

God sent his Son, Jesus, to die on the cross that you could be saved and have a new life.

See Romans 5:8 and John 10:10*

Design by Reba McBride Computerorbits

You can grow as a Christian:

❖ **Attend a Bible-believing church.**

❖ Read the Bible and learn about God and His principles. (Example: Start with the book of John, one chapter at a time.)

❖ Turn from sinful living.

❖ Pray often to God in Jesus' name—Talk to God. Confess your sins; share your joys and problems. Thank God for your blessings.

❖ Tell others about your Savior.

You are invited to:

Place your Ministry or Church name here and use it as your own.

Do
You
Know
for Sure?

You Can Know Jesus

Jesus said,

"I am the way, the truth, and the life. No one comes to the Father except through me. . ." (John 14:6)

". . . I stand at the door and knock. If you let me in, I will come in. . . ." (Revelation 3:20)

Would you like to invite Jesus into your heart --- Right now?

Just say, "Lord Jesus, come into my heart. Be my Lord and my Savior."

1 Believe in your heart: that Jesus Christ is the Son of God; that He died for you on the cross; that he rose from the dead.

2 Then confess with your mouth that Jesus is your Lord and Savior.

3 You will be saved.

Romans10:9: If you confess with your mouth the Lord Jesus, and believe in your heart that God has raised him from the dead, you will be saved.

You can know for sure where you're going when you die.

God loves you and wants you to know that you're going to heaven when you die.

Everyone has sinned and come short of the glory of God. Sin has separated us from God.

Romans 3:23: For all have sinned, and come short of the glory of God.

God sent his Son, Jesus, to die on the cross that you could be saved and have a new life.

See Romans 5:8 and John 10:10*

Design by Reba McBride Computerorbits

You can grow as a Christian:

❖ **Attend a Bible-believing church.**

❖ Read the Bible and learn about God and His principles.

(Example: Start with the book of John, one chapter at a time.)

❖ Turn from sinful living.

❖ Pray often to God in Jesus' name—Talk to God. Confess your sins; share your joys and problems. Thank God for your blessings.

❖ Tell others about your Savior.

You are invited to:

Place your Ministry or Church name here and use it as your own.

Permission is granted by the author to copy and use this "Do You Know for Sure?" brochure for ministry and personal use. Please do not reprint for commercial use or resale.

Copyright © 2006
Barbara Walker Sowersby
International Outreach Ministries
Tulsa, Oklahoma

Do
You
Know
for Sure?

You Can Know Jesus

Jesus said,

"I am the way, the truth, and the life. No one comes to the Father except through me. . ." (John 14:6)

". . . I stand at the door and knock. If you let me in, I will come in. . . ." (Revelation 3:20)

---

1 Believe in your heart:
that Jesus Christ is the Son of God;
that He died for you on the cross;
that he rose from the dead.

2 Then confess with your mouth
that Jesus is your Lord and Savior.

3 You will be saved.

Romans 10:9: If you confess with your mouth the Lord Jesus, and believe in your heart that God has raised him from the dead, you will be saved.

Would you like to invite Jesus into your heart --- **Right now?**

Just say, **"Lord Jesus, come into my heart. Be my Lord and my Savior."**

You can know **for sure** where you're going when you die.

God loves you and wants you to know that you're going to heaven when you die.

Everyone has sinned and come short of the glory of God.
Sin has separated us from God.

Romans 3:23: For all have sinned, and come short of the glory of God.

God sent his Son, Jesus, to die on the cross that you could be saved and have a new life.

See Romans 5:8 and John 10:10*

Design by Reba McBride Computerorbits